A New True Book

DAIRY COWS

By Kathy Henderson

CHILDRENS PRESS ®

CHICAGO

Purebred Jersey

In memory of Twister, No. R24
1978 - 1988

PHOTO CREDITS

©Cameramann International, Ltd.—4 (bottom), 28, (2 photos), 36, 37, 39 (2 photos), 41, 42 (4 photos), 43 (2 photos), 44 (2 photos)

Journalism Services:
©Ruth Ann Angus—25 (top)
©Paul Burd—25 (bottom right)
©Paul Gero—33 (top)
©Steve Sumner—10 (left)

Root Resources:
©Ray F. Hillstrom—17 (left)
©Russel Kreite—27 (left)
©Lia E. Munson—45
©Kenneth Rapalee—9 (right), 15 (left), 33 (bottom), 35

©James Rowan—8 (left), 14 (left), 31

Lynn Stone—Cover, 2, 4 (top), 6, 7, 8 (right), 9 (left), 10 (right), 12 (2 photos), 13, 14 (right), 15 (right), 21, 22, 23, 25 (bottom left), 27 (right), 30

Charles Hills, 18

Cover—Purebred Guernsey cows

Library of Congress Cataloging-in-Publication Data

Henderson, Kathy.
  Dairy cows / by Kathy Henderson.
    p.   cm. — (A New true book)
  Includes index.
  Summary: Describes the physical characteristics and life cycle of dairy cows, how milk is made, the use of milking machines, and the processing of raw milk at the dairy plant.
  ISBN 0-516-01152-9
  1. Dairy cattle—Juvenile literature. 2. Dairy farming—Juvenile literature. [1. Dairy cattle. 2. Cows. 3. Dairying. 4. Milk.]
  I. Title.
SF208.H46 1988   88-11123
636.2'142—dc19   CIP
                            AC

TABLE OF CONTENTS

Holstein cows head for the barn and patiently
wait to be let into the milking barn.

DAIRY COWS

"Here, Bossie," a farmer calls. One by one, cows rise to their feet. They head for the barn to be milked.

"Bossie" is a nickname for dairy cows. It comes from an old Latin term, *Bos taurus*, which means ox. Some farmers use this nickname to call their cows in from pasture.

Holsteins are black and white.

There are many kinds of dairy cows. Holsteins are black and white. They are the most popular dairy cows, because they give the most milk.

Jerseys are brown.

Jersey cows are light brown. Their milk is rich in butterfat. It is best for making butter and cheese.

7

Ayrshires (above) and
Guernseys (right)

Ayrshires came from
Scotland. They are red or
brown with white spots.
Guernsey cows can be
yellow, brown, or red
colored.

Most Brown Swiss cows
live in Switzerland. They

Brown Swiss bulls (right)
are bigger than the cows.

are used for both beef
and milk.

Dairy cows weigh as
much as 1500 pounds.
Bulls are even bigger.

A dairy cow can give
about five gallons of milk

each day. In one year, a good cow might give over 2,000 gallons of milk!

Despite their size, dairy cows are gentle animals. They like to be petted and talked to.

HEAD TO TAIL

Most dairy cows grow horns. Some horns are short and curved. Others are long and sharp.

Horns can be dangerous to people as well as to other cows. Most farmers remove horns when they are little so they will not grow. This hurts the cow only a little bit.

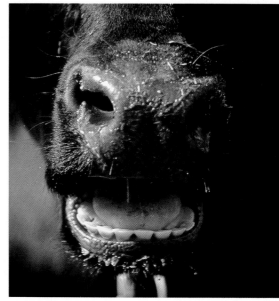

These Holstein calves (left) have recently had their
horns cut off. Close-up of a cow's muzzle and teeth (right)

A cow's nose has tiny
drops of moisture on it.
The moisture helps the
cow taste its food.

Unlike a horse, a cow
has teeth only on its
bottom jaw at the front of
its mouth. In the back of

Purebred Guernseys in their barn

its mouth, it has large molars, both top and bottom. These help a cow grind tough hay and grain.

The bag where milk is stored is called an "udder." It hangs between the cow's back legs. An

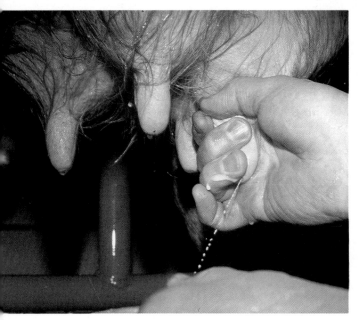

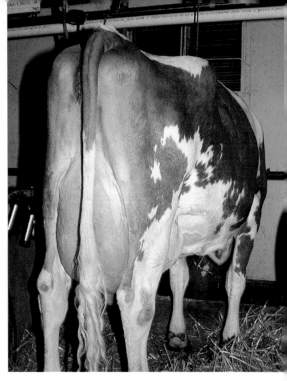

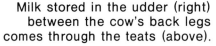
Milk stored in the udder (right)
between the cow's back legs
comes through the teats (above).

udder has four nipples
called "teats," where the
milk comes out.

A cow's foot, or "hoof,"
is always growing.
Sometimes a farmer
scrapes the bottom of a

14

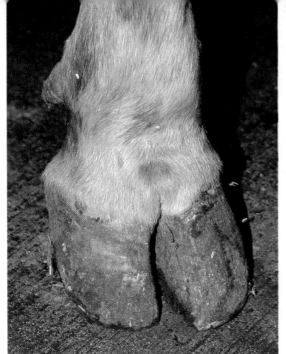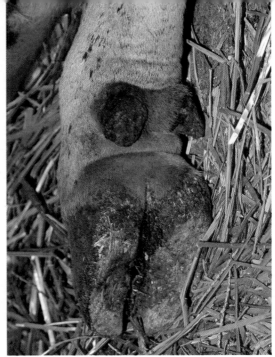

Front of hoof (left) and back of hoof (right)

cow's hoof with a rasp. A rasp is like a big, steel fingernail file. This scraping keeps the hoof from growing too long.

A cow's long tail helps swish flies away in summer.

DIGESTIVE SYSTEM

The way a cow eats is different from most other animals. A cow eats very fast. It only chews food enough to swallow it. Later, it will rest and "chew its cud." It will burp up small amounts of food to chew again.

Dairy cows eat about 50 pounds of food each day. They like hay and corn

Holsteins eat about 50 pounds of food each day.

and oats. Some farmers
also feed cows other grains
and silage. Cows are fed
salt, vitamins, and minerals
to keep them healthy.

A cow drinks at least 15
gallons of water each day.

17

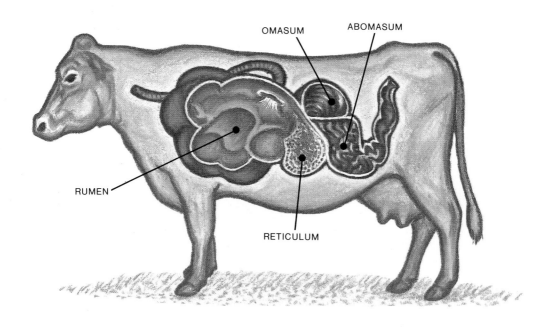

OMASUM   ABOMASUM

RUMEN

RETICULUM

A cow's stomach is divided into four parts. When a cow eats, the food goes into the "rumen" and the "reticulum." After a cow chews her cud, the food goes down into the parts of the stomach called the "omasum" and "abomasum" where it is finally digested.

Part of the food helps the cow grow and stay healthy. Some of it makes milk in the udder. Any undigested food is expelled from the cow as "manure" or turned into body fat.

Farmers use manure to fertilize the soil. Nothing that the cow eats is wasted.

CALVES AND HEIFERS

A cow cannot make milk until it has a baby. After a cow mates with a bull, it will take nine months for the baby to be born. A baby cow is called a calf.

A cow will give milk until two months before she has her next calf. Then the farmer will "dry her up" by milking her only once a day and then not at all.

A calf can stand soon after it is born. It will drink

A Guernsey calf drinks its mother's special milk.

a special milk (colostrum)
made by its mother.

The special milk is extra
rich in proteins, and
vitamins. It also has

antibodies which protect the calf from diseases.

Gradually, the cow will produce regular milk.

Baby dairy calves do not stay with their mothers for long. They are moved to

A pen, or calf hutch, separates this mother from her calf.

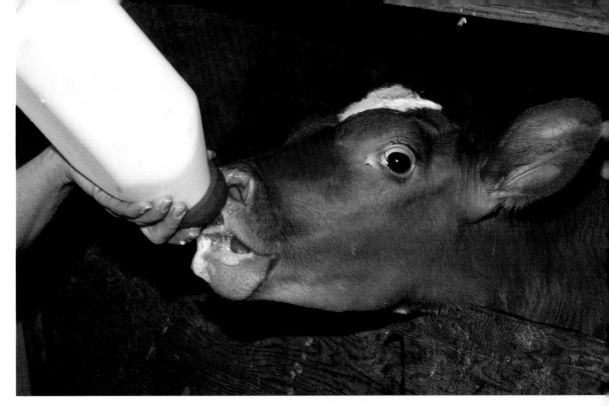

Guernsey calf drinks from its special bottle.

special pens or calf hutches
so they do not drink all
their mother's milk.

Calves are fed warm
milk from bottles with large
nipples. Soon they will be
nibbling hay and grain.

Bull calves are usually sold to other farmers to raise. Later, they may be used for breeding, or for producing veal or beef.

A female calf is called a heifer. After a heifer is two or three years old, she is able to have her first baby. Then she will be called a cow.

Herefords, such as the bull shown above, are raised for their beef. The Guernsey (below left) and the Holsteins (below right with a newborn calf) are raised for their milk.

HOW MILK IS MADE

Milk is made from nutrients in the cow's bloodstream. It collects in the udder in thousands of tiny sacs called "alveoli."

Each of the cow's teats has many sets of milk sacs. They are connected to the teat by small tubes called milk ducts. When a teat is pulled and gently squeezed, milk flows down the duct and out each teat.

Farmers must keep the cows and milk clean. Before milking, they carefully wash each teat. After milking, the teats are wiped dry.

Farmers work hard to keep their dairy cows clean and healthy.

Milking barn (above) in Plymouth, New Zealand
When a cow's udder is full (below), it becomes swollen.

Cows are milked twice each day. They are milked once in the morning. They are milked again in the evening.

If a cow is not milked on time, her udder will become sore and swollen. She may get a disease called "mastitis." Then her milk will not be good to drink.

DAIRY BARNS AND EQUIPMENT

A long time ago farmers milked their cows by hand. It was hard work and took a long time.

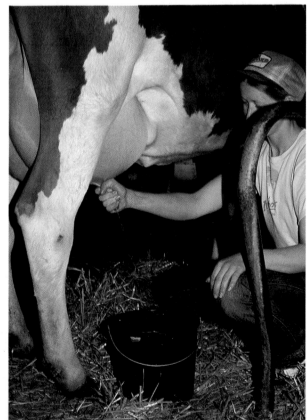

Very few farmers milk cows by hand anymore.

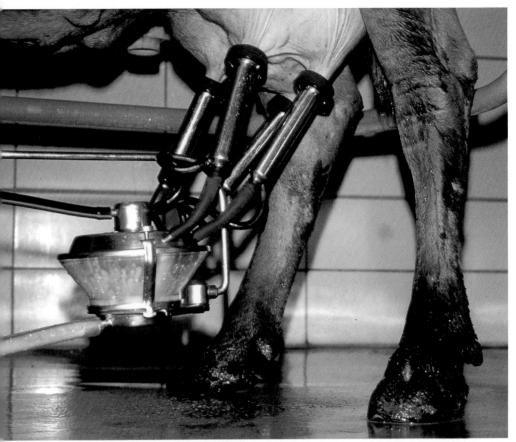

Modern dairy
farms use
milking
machines.

Today farmers use
milking machines. The
machines are connected to
a vacuum pump that pulls
and squeezes the teats
just like a calf sucking.

Some farmers keep cows in a stanchion barn. This kind of barn has special frames called stanchions that loosely hold a cow's head while she is being milked. The farmer carries the milking machine with him as he goes from cow to cow.

The cows can eat, drink, and sleep while held in their stanchions. Each stall is filled with straw or

Stanchions (above) are used to keep a cow's head in place. The cows do not seem to mind.

sawdust in winter to keep the cows warm and comfortable.

Some farmers milk cows in a milking parlor. The farmer stands in a shallow pit with the milking machines. The cows come into the parlor to be milked then go out again. Cows eat, drink, and sleep in different parts of the barn, called freestalls.

Milk travels from the cow through hoses to the pipeline that leads to the farm's storage tank.

Milk from milking machines goes directly from the cow into the bulk tank. It travels through a hose connected to the milking machine and the pipeline. The pipeline is connected to the bulk tank. No one ever touches the milk. It stays clean and sanitary.

The bulk tank is in a separate room called the milk house. The tank cools the warm milk right away. The milk must be kept below 40°F to keep it fresh.

Huge tank trucks pipe milk from the bulk tanks. Like the cows, these tanks must be kept clean and free from germs.

Tank truck delivers milk to a dairy.

FROM FARM TO YOU

A large tank truck comes to the farm to pick up the raw milk and take it to the dairy plant for processing.

Like the bulk tank, the tank truck will keep the milk cool and sanitary.

The driver will take a sample of milk from the farmer's bulk tank before pumping the milk into the truck. Laboratory technicians at the dairy plant will test the sample to be sure the milk is safe to drink.

Laboratory technicians (below) at the dairy test the milk samples before the milk is processed.

At the dairy plant the milk will be pumped into large vats with milk from other dairy farms.

The milk will be pasteurized by heating it to kill any disease-causing bacteria and to keep it from spoiling. It will also be homogenized so all the globules in the butterfat

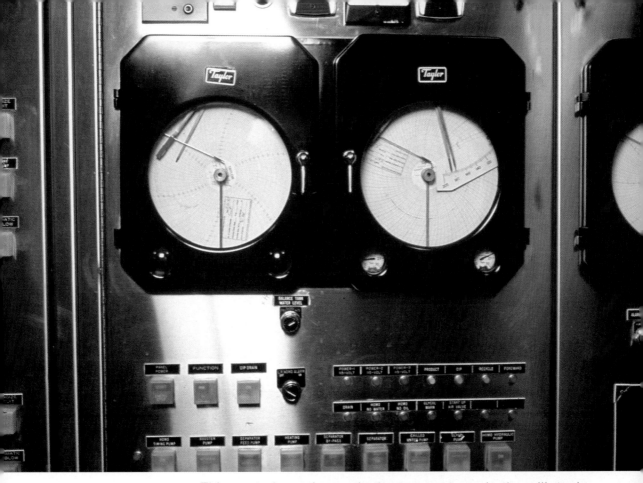

This control panel records the temperatures in the milk tanks.
Milk is heated to kill any disease-causing bacteria it might have.

are broken down into the same size. Homogenizing makes milk and other dairy products easier to digest.

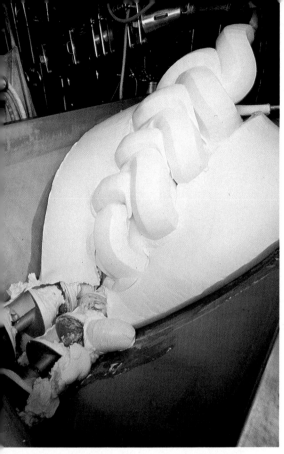
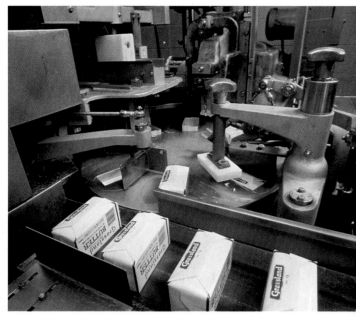

Huge machines are used to churn butter (top left) and mold it into one pound packs (top right). Machines also are used to process and mold swiss cheese (below).

Cheese and ice cream are two favorite foods made from milk.

Some of the creamy butterfat in the milk will be removed to make other products, such as butter, cheese, and whipping cream.

Containers of white milk (above) and chocolate milk (right) are filled by machine.

Although they are lying down, these cows are working.
They are making milk for everyone.

The rest of the milk will be packaged in cartons and plastic jugs.

Trucks pick up all the different milk products and deliver them to your favorite store for you to buy and enjoy.

WORDS YOU SHOULD KNOW

abomasum(ab • oh • MASS • um) — fourth part of a cow's stomach

alveoli(al • vee • OH • lee) — tiny groups of cells in cow's udder where milk is made

antibodies(AN • tee • bah • deez) — natural proteins which help prevent disease

Bossie(BOSS • ee) (BAW • see) — nickname for calf or cow

butterfat(BUT • er • fat) — the fatty particles in milk that make butter and cheese

colostrum(kuh • LAWSS • trum) — first milk made by cow for its calf

cud(CUHD) — food that a cow swallows then brings back up to finish chewing

expel(ex • PEL) — to force out

fertilize(FER • tih • lize) — to add nutrients to the soil to help plants grow

freestalls(FREE • stawlz) — open areas in a barn where cows can move around freely to eat or rest

grain(GRAYN) — the seed of the wheat, corn, oats or other cereal plants

hay(HAY) — special types of grasses which are cut, dried and stored as feed for animals

healthy(HELTH • ee) — to be in good condition; to be normal

heifer(HEFF • er) — a young female cow

homogenize(huh • MAHJ • in • ize) — a process that breaks down the drops of fat in milk into tiny particles

hoof(HOOF) — the foot of a cow or horse

incisor(IN • size • er) — a front tooth

manure(ma • NOOR) — waste matter expelled from an animal

mastitis(mass • TYE • tiss) — a disease of the udder

molar(MOH • ler) — a back tooth

nutrients(NOO • tree • ents) — good things in food that help an animal grow and stay healthy

omasum(o • MAH • sum) — third part of a cow's stomach

parlor(PAR • ler) — type of dairy barn where cows are milked

pasteurize(PASS • cher • ize) — a process which uses heat to kill bacteria in raw milk

raw milk(RAW MIHLK) — milk that has not been pasteurized

reticulum(reh • TICK • yoo • lum) — second part of a cow's stomach

rumen(ROO • min) — first part of a cow's stomach

sanitary(SAN • ih • tair • ee) — to keep clean and free of bacteria

silage(SYE • lij) — hay or corn cut while still green and stored in silos for animal feed

stanchion(STAN • chyun) — an upright frame that loosely holds a cow's head while she stands in place to be milked

straw(STRAW) — the dried yellow stalks of oat or wheat plants used for bedding animal stalls

teat(TEET) — the nipple part of an udder

udder(UH • der) — part of the cow where milk is made and stored

INDEX

About the Author

Kathy Henderson is Executive Director of the National Association for Young Writers, vice president of the NAYW Board of Trustees, and Michigan Advisor for the Society of Children's Book Writers. She works closely with children, teachers, and librarians through young author conferences and workshops, and is a frequent guest speaker in schools. An experienced freelance writer with hundreds of newspaper and magazine articles to her credit, she is also the author of the Market Guide for Young Writers. *Mrs. Henderson lives on a 400-acre dairy farm in Michigan with her husband, Keith, and two teenage children.*